THE WORLD'S GREATEST LEFT-HANDERS

THE WORLD'S GREATEST LEFT-HANDERS

WHY LEFT-HANDERS ARE JUST PLAIN BETTER THAN EVERYBODY ELSE

JAMES T. de KAY and SANDY HUFFAKER

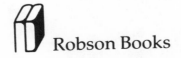

Robson Books

First published in Great Britain in 1995 by
Robson Books Ltd, Bolsover House, 5-6 Clipstone
Street, London W1P 8LE

British Library Cataloguing in Publication Data
A catalogue record for this title is available from
the British Library

ISBN 0 86051 996 1

Design by Diane Gedymin

Printed in Finland by WSOY

If you are left-handed, this book is dedicated to you.
If you aren't, eat your heart out.

Left-handers are a different breed . . .

TYPICAL
RIGHT-HANDER

They really are.

TYPICAL
LEFT-HANDER

THE BRAIN

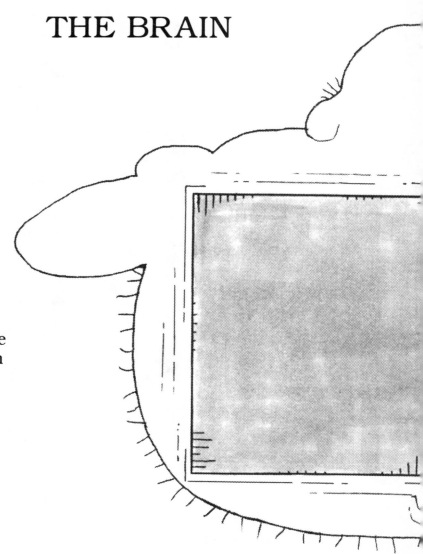

Right-handers are wired
into the logical half of the
brain, which makes them
sensible,
reasonable,
and dull.

(AERIAL VIEW)

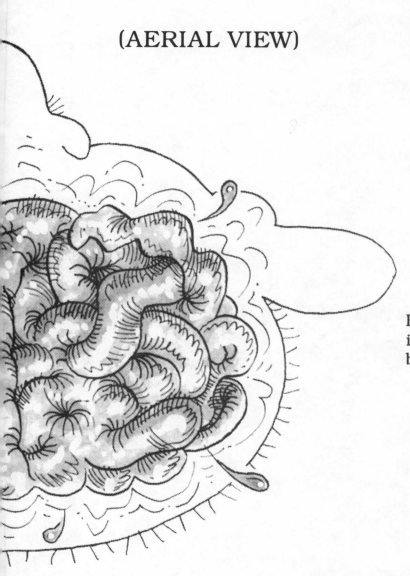

But left-handers are wired
into the artistic half of the
brain, which makes them
imaginative,
creative,
surprising,
ambiguous,
exasperating,
stubborn,
emotional,
witty,
obsessive,
infuriating,
delightful,
original,
but never, *never* dull.

The goofy, unpredictable nature of left-handers is why so many of them turn out to be great achievers, including the assortment of saints, scallywags, heroes, wackos, and geniuses in the following pages....

BUZZ ALDRIN

The record of left-handers in the space program is highly significant. Of the twelve astronauts who actually walked on the moon, four were left-handed. That's one in three, compared to a national average of one left-hander in ten. Obviously left-handers, with their recognized capacity for original thought, intuition, and self-reliance, are particularly suited to the rigors of space travel.

Buzz Aldrin was the first of the left-handers on the moon, His initial task, after climbing from the lunar module, was to take a picture of his captain, Neil Armstrong, with a Hasselblad camera—one of the most right-handed bits of machinery ever invented.

ALEXANDER THE GREAT

Left-handedness is more than just a physical specialization. It's a state of mind. And no example proves it better than one of the earliest recorded left-handers, Alexander of Macedon. He was a warrior, visionary, world leader, and crybaby, all wrapped up in a single, immensely complicated package. In a lifetime of only thirty-three years he created the first modern empire, invented snorkel diving, designed the first planned city, and cut the Gordian knot, whatever that was.

His like will never be seen again because, like all left-handers, he was a true original.

CARL PHILIPP EMANUEL BACH

Johann Sebastian Bach had twenty children, many of whom made a living in the music business. By far the most successful was his second son, the left-handed C.P.E. Bach, whose compositions were actually more popular than his father's (Johann Sebastian was not amused).

It's likely that quite a number of Bach's family were left-handed (the trait is closely related to musical talent), but Germanic culture has always been strongly biased against the left hand, and C.P.E. may have been the only Bach who wasn't forcibly switched to right-handedness. Although switching has been shown to cause serious psychological consequences (including stammering), it is still common in Germany, although it has largely disappeared elsewhere.

PETER BENCHLEY

The author of *Jaws* may be the most determinedly right-handed left-hander on record. The fact is, Peter Benchley favors his right hand for virtually all activities—playing tennis, throwing a ball, hammering a nail, etc. The only exception is writing, which he does left-handedly. To a neurologist this makes him left-handed. He may be right-handed at virtually everything else, but the act of writing is so difficult, so complex, so significant a skill that it far outweighs any other manifestation of handedness. If you write left-handed, you *are* left-handed, and that's that.

700 BENJAMITES

The Bible is militantly right-handed and takes every opportunity to equate left-handedness with evil (literally, a lack of righteousness). The sole exception to this prejudice seems to be in the Book of Judges, which includes the story of the seven hundred left-handed Benjamites who chased the Israelite army off the field of battle.

The Arabs have been trying to learn their secret for years.

BILLY THE KID

The murderous William H. Bonney, who was born in Brooklyn, had shot twenty-one men by the time he was twenty-one years old. And he killed them all left-handedly. Chances are he was left-eyed as well, because he had to be a good shot to compile a record like that. (You can be left-eyed, left-eared, and left-footed as well as left-handed. It's usually more efficient to keep your dominances on the same side of the body.)

Billy died in New Mexico before he was twenty-two, which is probably why he's still known as Billy the Kid instead of Billy the Grown-up.

CAROL BURNETT

You'd think left-handers would be a pretty gloomy bunch, considering the number of booby traps the world sets out for them—right-handed scissors, right-handed golf clubs, right-handed can openers, etc. But instead of crying about their fate, left-handers are more likely to turn into comedians. Carol Burnett is only one of a long, long list of distinguished left-handers who make a living by making you laugh.

Why so many left-handed comics? There seems to be something goofy about the way they look at the world. Maybe they see it a little more clearly.

LEWIS CARROLL

Charles Dodgson, who called himself Lewis Carroll and created Alice in Wonderland, exhibits all the earmarks of a left-hander switched to right-handedness: stammering, extreme shyness, and a sort of controlled dyslexia that takes the form of punning and other word play, mirror writing, and a kind of humor that depends on spectacularly unreasonable reasoning.

Certainly *Through the Looking-Glass*, with its wrong-way-around orientation, its loony logic, and its mind-warping Jabberwocky, is the greatest left-handed masterpiece in literature.

CHARLIE CHAPLIN

And then there's Charlie Chaplin. With a cane, a pasted-on moustache, and a few bits of clothing picked up from Mack Sennett's wardrobe, he created a character that can still bring tears of laughter to the world.

Significantly, the left-handed brain is not only unpredictable (which is why it's so comical), but also nonverbal (which is why Chaplin and several other people in this book managed to communicate so well without words).

CHARLEMAGNE

Charlemagne was King of the Franks and eventually the first Emperor in Western Europe. He did all the things expected of a great leader: he fought wars, gave parties, and fooled around with women.

He was also illiterate, which suited his left-handedness just fine. Left-handers have always had trouble with our left-to-right style of writing (they can't see what they've written until they take their hand away). Being illiterate gave Charlemagne more time to fight, party, and fool around with women.

JIMMY CONNORS

Tennis has traditionally been a magnet for left-handers, and recently they have come to dominate both the men's and women's divisions. The terrible-tempered Jimmy Connors, who has insulted umpires and ball boys on five continents, is typical of the breed.

Just why so many left-handers should be drawn to tennis probably stems from the fact that left-handers tend (a) to be loners rather than team players, and (b) to have particularly well developed space perception. Tennis, with its need for individual action and precise aim, fits them to a T.

GENTLEMAN JIM CORBETT

The man who won the heavyweight crown from the great John L. Sullivan in New Orleans in 1892 did so primarily with the aid of his left fist. Corbett remained the only great left-handed prizefighter until Carmen Basilio came on the scene in 1955. The fact that left-handers have not distinguished themselves to any great extent in the manly art of self-defense does not necessarily mean they are cowardly by nature. But it may indicate an innate lack of bellicosity.

BOB DYLAN

Musical composition came incredibly easily to Bob Dylan, the left-handed singer. He wrote the intensely melodic tune to "Blowin' in the Wind" in less than five minutes, while the words took him almost a month of effort.

As noted elsewhere, the left-handed brain handles music effortlessly but is apt to have some difficulty with language.

M. C. ESCHER

Mathematicians, critics, and teenagers are all admirers of the drawings and engravings of M. C. Escher, the remarkable Dutch artist who could convince you that water flowed upstream and architecture had four dimensions. Escher attributed his highly specialized skills to his left-handedness.

The Escher engravings, found today everywhere from textbooks to T-shirts, demonstrate a highly logical form of illogic, an intellectual approach to the impossible, a fascination with alternative worlds. They also represent a highly civilized horselaugh, which is the left-handed brain in action.

BENJAMIN FRANKLIN

The left-handedness of America's greatest wit, diplomat, scientist, and publisher helped him in his early career as a printer, because left-handers come naturally to a very unusual skill: the ability to read and write backwards. In Franklin's day a printer had to set type by hand, and it was a distinct asset to be able to read the type, which was, of course, in reverse.

This backwards-reading skill, which all typesetters pick up, comes easily to left-handers, who have an innate preference for reading right to left. The tendency to read the wrong way accounts for the large number of left-handed dyslexics.

GRETA GARBO

Greta Garbo, the greatest movie star of all time, was most famous for a single line of dialogue: "I vant to be alone." The line relates to her reclusive nature—she was always painfully shy—and also to her left-handedness. In general, because the left-handed brain is nonverbal, left-handers are often not good talkers and are apt to avoid social contact.

Garbo, who established herself before talking films, is one of the many left-handers who were superb silent communicators.

JUDY GARLAND

For some thirty years, Judy Garland reigned supreme as one of the world's greatest singers and actresses. From child star to torch singer, she touched hearts around the world in a way that has never been equaled. The fact that she was left-handed helps explain how she was able to project such a remarkable sense of fragility and vulnerability, because these are characteristics of the slightly out-of-phase nature of left-handers.

URI GELLER

Uri Geller continues to fascinate people by bending spoons, etc., using only sheer mental concentration. Whether the left-handed Geller is a charlatan or a natural wonder, his mental gymnastics are typical of left-handed thinking. . . . Unorthodox ways of thought are absolutely standard among left-handers.

GEORGE VI

King George VI, one of the multitudinous left-handed members of the Royal family (his widow, Elizabeth, the Queen Mother, is also left-handed, as is their grandson the Prince of Wales), was trained into right-handedness as a child. As a direct result, he suffered from a serious s-s-s-peech im-p-pediment his entire life.

Luckily, his unfortunate disability did not preclude him from finding gainful employment as an adult.

WHOOPI GOLDBERG

Whoopi Goldberg may be the only Oscar winner named after a cushion. That would be reason enough to qualify her as one of the great left-handers, but she has such a dazzling off-the-wall personality she'd have made the list even if her name was Jane Smith. It's the surprise factor that makes left-handers so interesting, and with Whoopi, her unpredictability is clearly of world class proportions.

CARY GRANT

In the film *Night and Day*, Cary Grant played the part of Cole Porter. Since Cole Porter was short, lame, and American, while Cary Grant was tall, fit, and English, he was obviously picked for the role because, like Porter, he was left-handed.

Except for the fact that he *is* left-handed, there is nothing particularly left-handed about Cary Grant's personality except, perhaps, for his devastating charm.

JIMI HENDRIX

Jimi Hendrix took his left-handedness lightly. He would either restring a right-handed guitar so he could play it left-handedly, or he'd play a right-handed guitar upside down without restringing it, or he'd play it backwards. He didn't care, and anyway, his wah-wah pedal was just as important as the guitar. He was a master musician, one of the many left-handed ones.

JIM HENSON

It takes a very special kind of person to create something as unique as the Muppets—someone with a gift of fantasy, humor, visual imagination, and that very special duality of personality that lets them be simultaneously themselves and another character. Not surprisingly, the man who fits that description and did in fact create the Muppets, Jim Henson, was left-handed.

It's worth noticing that Kermit the Frog, his first and foremost Muppet, is also left-handed (check the way he holds the banjo).

BEN HOGAN

When the left-handed Ben Hogan started playing golf as a kid in Texas, he had to swing right-handed with a set of clubs borrowed from a friend. As he began to make a name for himself in the sport, he considered switching to left-handed clubs, but was dissuaded by "experts" who told him that his natural left-handedness gave his right-handed swing extra power. He took their advice, but years later, after his retirement, he regretted that he hadn't made the switch in his youth.

JACK THE RIPPER

When the precarious balance of the left-handed brain goes out of whack, the results can be disastrous—witness Jack the Ripper, the terror of Victorian London. All his victims were women, murdered with identical mutilations, clearly of a psychosexual nature. Who was he? Scotland Yard had only one clue: the knife wounds clearly showed the Ripper was left-handed. The clue was significant, for in nineteenth-century England only 2 percent of the population was left-handed (compared to around 10 percent today). Even so, the Ripper was never found.

Interestingly enough, the case was never closed. Recently suspicion has come to rest on the left-handed Duke of Clarence, grandson of Queen Victoria, which may explain why the police records of the murders are still under lock and key, protected by the Official Secrets Act.

JOAN OF ARC

Joan of Arc heard voices. This unschooled peasant girl believed she could save France, and she convinced the King to give her control of his army. Miraculous? Sure, but also very left-handed. Both the hearing of internal voices and the strong feelings of invincible superiority are closely associated with the left-handed brain. Further proof of Joan's left-handedness is that the only contemporary sketch of her shows her holding her sword in her left hand.

LEONARDO DA VINCI

There are left-handers and there are left-handers. And then there's Leonardo da Vinci, who was so left-handed he needs some special category of his own. He is the patron saint of the breed, and with good reason. He not only invented left-handed machines, painted left-handed masterpieces, and created left-handed statues, he also wrote left-handed—that is, he wrote backwards, from right to left, because that's the sensible way for a left-hander to do it. Of course, this mirror writing was a little difficult for other people to read, but Leo couldn't have cared less.

SHIRLEY MacLAINE

Oscar-winner Shirley MacLaine gives evidence of her left-handedness at every turn. She's a dancer (left-handers have a special thing about music). She's a best-selling writer (left-handers are naturally creative). And she's spent the better part of her life portraying an astonishing parade of kooks (and no one understands kooks better than left-handers).

MARCEL MARCEAU

It's not surprising that the world's greatest mime is left-handed. Indeed, it would be surprising if he weren't. Marcel Marceau's left-handed brain may be nonverbal, but it can speak volumes with the twitch of an eyebrow, a shrug, or the curl of a lip. As he and the other left-handed mimes in this book will attest, if you've got something to say, words may be the least effective way to express it.

HARPO MARX

The Marx Brothers' comedy trademark was uproarious anarchy, and while madness might emanate from any one of them, it was the left-handed Harpo who was undoubtedly the maddest of the bunch. He was, of course, the nonverbal one, too, using his left-handed body language to drown out Groucho and Chico.

PAUL McCARTNEY

Paul McCartney, who plays bass left-handedly and can write a hit song as easily as most people cross the street, is something of a left-handed puzzle. Certainly his handedness and his music go together, but McCartney also exhibits characteristics almost never found in left-handers, including a high degree of business sophistication and a reasonableness and level-headedness generally associated with right-handers. Somehow he breaks the pattern, but perhaps he is proof of just how different left-handers can be . . . even from each other.

MICHELANGELO BUONARROTI

Like Leonardo, Michelangelo is another of those left-handed Florentine artists who seemed to dominate the Italian Renaissance. He's further proof of the strong artistic influence of the left-handed brain: the visionary who could comprehend and solve the enormous technical problems of St. Peter's dome, as well as the obsessive personality who could spend nearly four years flat on his back painting the ceiling.

MARILYN MONROE

There were other, more beautiful movie stars and other, greater actresses. Her list of screen credits is remarkably short of distinguished films. But decades after her death by sleeping pills, Marilyn Monroe continues to cast a spell, to capture the imagination of millions. Whatever she had—and she certainly had something—is impossible to define with any precision, other than to say it was unique.

The fact that she was left-handed—that she shared the sometimes fragile, kooky, surprising nature common to left-handedness—is an important clue to this remarkable woman.

NAPOLEON BONAPARTE

Napoleon never seemed to know what to do with his right hand, and kept it stuck in his vest for the most part. Some people figured he was scratching fleas, but the fact was he was left-handed (although he'd been switched as a child).

His left-handed character surfaced in his quirky imagination, his astonishing vision, his brilliant insight, and his harebrained scheme to conquer Russia.

MARTINA NAVRATILOVA

Former Wimbledon champion Navratilova is another of those left-handers who dominated world tennis. Left-handedness is twice as common among males as among females, which may account for the fact that Martina had fewer left-handed competitors than did Connors, McEnroe, etc.

VISCOUNT HORATIO NELSON

The left-handed Lord Nelson is perhaps history's greatest naval officer, known for his daring, his imagination, and his ability to surprise the enemy. But before we credit all his genius to his left-handedness, it should be noted that he came by it the hard way: he was by nature right-handed, but switched over when his right arm was blown off in the Battle of Tenerife.

PELÉ

Edson Arantes do Nascimento, the great Brazilian soccer player better known as Pelé, is left-handed. This fact may not seem particularly significant in a sport where you aren't allowed to handle the ball, but what makes it important is that he's also left-footed (most left-handers are) and can kick from the port side with a strength and accuracy most players can't even manage from starboard.

COLE PORTER

At an early age, Cole Porter showed a strong preference for doing things left-handedly. Fortunately, the young Cole had enlightened parents who didn't try to switch him to right-handedness. As a result he grew up and wrote lots of hit songs, including "I Get a Kick Out of You," "Boola-Boola," and "You're the Top."

The left-handed brain is the centre of both the sense of rhythm and the perception of pitch, which explains why so many composers and musicians are left-handed.

RICHARD PRYOR

Almost every good comedian is highly complex, and Richard Pryor is one of the best and one of the most complicated. It's not surprising he's left-handed, too. His ambiguous personality (sometimes he plays the frightened tough guy, sometimes he's just the opposite—the vengeful coward), combined with a wildly funny sense of the ridiculous, marks him as a typically outrageous, unpredictable, original left-hander.

RAMSES II

The left-handed Pharaoh Ramses II, who built temples and monuments to himself from Karnak to Abu Simbel, is best remembered for turning a deaf ear to the requests of Moses. As a result, his kingdom suffered a series of misfortunes including a plague of locusts, an inundation of frogs, an epidemic of boils, and various other inconveniences. Finally, to top it all off, his entire army was drowned in the Red Sea.

Stubbornness, to the point of downright unreasonableness is often characteristic of left-handers.

NORMAN SCHWARZKOPF

General Schwarzkopf's left-handedness is one reason he's got so many stars on his uniform. A good military commander has to be able to see the battle from many different points of view simultaneously—he has to perceive the constantly changing capabilities of his different units, grasp what the enemy is up to, and understand the problems facing the soldiers, sailors, and fliers under his command. Because the general's left-handed brain thinks holistically, he can make all sorts of different judgement calls simultaneously. In the war with Iraq, the bombs were smart, but the commander was smarter.

MARK SPITZ

Mark Spitz, who won seven gold medals in the 1972 Olympics, represents a very special aspect of left-handedness: its strong relationship to swimming.

The left-handed brain is the seat of visual perception and spacial analysis, which means left-handers are apt to have a better than average sense of sight. Water sports require extra work on the part of the eyes, which must constantly adjust to the radically different optical conditions above and below the surface. Since left-handers can handle this problem with greater ease, they are more apt to be drawn to water sports. Their small but real advantage accounts for the high percentage of left-handers on high school and college swimming teams.

RUDY VALLEE

Rudy Vallee, who carried on a blatantly open love affair with himself for over forty years of public life, was a left-handed singer, bandleader, and movie star. His ego was legend. He once petitioned the city of Los Angeles to get the street that he lived on renamed "Rue de Vallee," but the city fathers didn't share his adoration of himself, and the name of Sunset Boulevard remained unchanged.

Probably his weirdest accomplishment was mastering the saxophone, which is the most decidedly right-handed musical instrument in general use.

QUEEN VICTORIA

The high proportion of left-handers in the royal family can be traced to Queen Victoria, who was herself left-handed but was switched in childhood. It has been the heavy documentation of the royal family over the generations—the endless court records, diaries, memoirs, and official histories, which have included all sorts of details including handedness of various siblings and cousins–that has provided scientists with the chief evidence to support the argument that left-handedness is inheritable, and therefore of a genetic nature.

Thanks to Victoria, we know that left-handers are born, not made.